Pupil Book

6

Tara Lievesley • Deborah Herridge

Series editor **John Stringer**

Author team
Deborah Herridge and Tara Lievesley

Series editor
John Stringer

Acknowledgements
The publishers wish to thank the following for permission to reproduce photographs:
Front cover photograph: **Ardea London**
Back cover photographs: **Oxford Scientific Films Ltd** (top and centre left), **Science Photo Library** (centre and bottom)

Gareth Bowden – page 38 (bottom); **Trevor Clifford** – pages 50 (top), 51 (top), 52 (bottom), 72 (bottom), 76 (centre); **Corbis** – © Bettmann/CORBIS page 25 (centre), © James A. Sugar/CORBIS 50 (centre); **Jeff Edwards** – page 32 (bottom); **Chris Honeywell** – page 14 (top), 24 (top and centre); **KPT Power Photos** – page 15 (top); **Andrew Lambert** – page 30 (top), 42 (centre); **Oxford Scientific Films Ltd** – pages 5 (bottom), 7 (top), 11 (top), 12 (bottom), 13 (top), 14 (bottom), 16 (top and bottom), 17 (top and centre), 20 (top), 43 (centre), 59 (top and centre), 79 (bottom), 84 (centre), 85 (bottom); **Philip Parkhouse** – page 47 (bottom); **Science Photo Library** – pages 12 (top), 19 (bottom), 24 (bottom), 27 (bottom), 31 (top), 39 (centre), 48 (centre), 50 (bottom), 52 (centre), 53 (centre), 58 (centre and bottom), 64 (centre), 83 (bottom), 84 (bottom) 85 (top); **Roger Scruton** – page 43 (top); **Tony Tickle** – page 59 (bottom)

Every effort has been made to contact copyright holders of any material in this book.
Any omissions will be rectified in subsequent printings if notice is given to the publishers.

Photography by Chris Coggins, Micrographix – pages 6 (centre), 28 (bottom), 30 (bottom), 41 (bottom), 42 (bottom), 52 (top)

Heinemann Educational Publishers
Halley Court, Jordan Hill, Oxford, OX2 8EJ
a division of Harcourt Education Ltd

www.myprimary.co.uk
Help and support, plus the widest range of education solutions.

Heinemann is a registered trademark of Harcourt Education Ltd

First published 2003

06 05 04 03
10 9 8 7 6 5 4 3 2 1

ISBN 0 435 13399 3

Designed and typeset by **Aqua Design Partners**
Illustrated by **Mark Ruffle, Shelagh McNicholas, Jon Stuart, Chrome Dome Design** and **Aqua Design Partners**
Printed in Spain by **Edelvives, Zaragoza**

Contents

How to use this book

At the beginning of each unit there is a list of things you should already know or be able to do.

Think about this question. By the end of the unit you will know how to answer it.

This shows words in the unit that are important. Try to remember them.

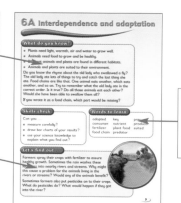

This box tells you what the lesson is about.

Try these activities. Your teacher will help you.

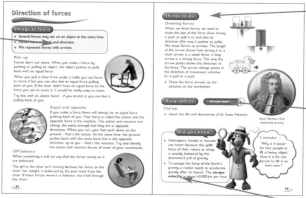

Use a CD-ROM to find out more. The colour shows which CD to use – **Life Processes**, **Materials** or **Physical Processes**.

Look out for safety tips!

This box tells you what you will find out during the lesson. Your teacher will help you.

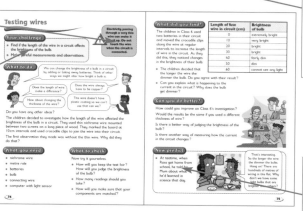

Find out what words in bold mean in the glossary at the back of the book.

Use what you have learned to answer these questions.

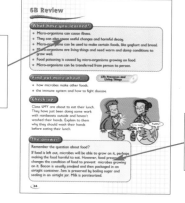

Check what you have learned in each unit.

Now answer the first question.

6A Interdependence and adaptation

What do you know?

- Plants need light, warmth, air and water to grow well.
- Animals need food to grow and be healthy.
- Different animals and plants are found in different habitats.
- Animals and plants are suited to their environment.

Do you know the rhyme about the old lady who swallowed a fly? The old lady ate lots of things to try and catch the last thing she ate. Food chains are like that. One animal eats another, which eats another, and so on. Try to remember what the old lady ate in the correct order. Is it true? Do all those animals eat each other? Would she have been able to swallow them all?

If you wrote it as a food chain, which part would be missing?

Skills check

Can you …

- measure carefully?
- draw bar charts of your results?
- use your science knowledge to explain what you find out?

Words to learn

adapted	key	prey
consumer	nutrient	producer
fertilizer	plant food	suited
food chain	predator	

Let's find out …

Farmers spray their crops with fertilizer to ensure healthy growth. Sometimes the rain washes these fertilizers into nearby rivers and streams. Why might this cause a problem for the animals living in the rivers or streams? Would any of the animals benefit?

Sometimes farmers also put pesticides on to their crops. What do pesticides do? What would happen if they got into the river?

Healthy plants

- Plants use light to make food and to grow well.
- Plants can grow without soil.
- Fertilizers provide additional nutrients to plants.

Are you 'green-fingered'?

This doesn't mean that you have the colour green on your fingers. It refers to whether you can look after plants well and keep them healthy when other people have failed. So do you think you have green fingers?

What do you think is wrong with the plant on the left? What would you do to make it more healthy? What do you think is wrong with the plant on the right? How do you know? What simple test could you do? How would you help it?

Bring me sunshine

You already know that plants need light to be able to grow well. You also know that seeds don't need light to germinate. Why? What does the growing plant need the light for? Plants use the energy from light to make their own food. This process is called **photosynthesis**. 'Photo' means 'light' and 'synthesis' means 'make'. They make sugars, and store them for future use as **starch**. They use this starch to make new leaves, stems and flowers. When we eat foods like potatoes and rice our bodies use the starch contained in them. Starch is a carbohydrate and is a necessary part of a well-balanced diet.

Multi-vitamins and minerals for plants

A healthy human diet should contain all the vitamins and minerals we need to stay well. But some humans boost their diet with extra vitamins – especially if they are unwell.

Plants draw all the minerals they need for healthy growth from the soil. But some soils are lacking in essential minerals. Plants may grow poorly in them – or not at all. Gardeners can boost plant growth with fertilizers. These contain the necessary nutrients. But what exactly are the plants getting?

The leaf is the plant's food factory

- Look at the backs of packets and bottles of plant 'foods' and fertilizers. Make a table of the ingredients. Are all products the same? Are some better for some plants than others?

Digging deeper

Cells and systems
Plant systems

Find out:

- more about photosynthesis.
- where photosynthesis takes place.

Did you know?

- During photosynthesis plants produce oxygen. Animals use this to breathe. A tree gives off enough oxygen in one year to keep four people alive!

- If you mark a tree 1m above the ground, your mark will always be 1m above the ground, no matter how tall the tree is. This is because all plants grow from their tips, not from their roots.

I wonder ...

If you give a tomato plant some 'house-plant food', would it help it grow better? Why?

Feeding plants

Your challenge

- Discover whether a plant needs nutrients added to its diet.
- Make careful measurements.

Are you feeling any better today?

Well, I've had plenty of water and sunlight, but I still feel weak.

What you need is a tonic — something like 'tomato feed'.

I don't know! Perhaps some new soil would be better?

What to do

One of these plants isn't growing well. It needs your 'green-fingered' touch. Before you try out your remedy on the sick plant, you should test your idea. This means you need to do some trials with healthy plants and see how they respond. You know what a plant needs to grow well. How do you make it really healthy? Here are some ideas.

I think you should re-pot the plant in new soil and give it tomato feed.

I think you should re-pot me in new soil. Then I will produce lots of new leaves.

I think you should give the plant tomato feed. This will make it grow strong and tall.

I think you should try another fertilizer.

What you need

- tomato feed and house-plant food
- new soil in the form of compost
- plant pots
- measuring cylinders
- a plastic squeeze pipette
- a tray of similar-sized tomato seedlings

What to check

Now try it yourselves.

- How will you know a plant has grown well? What observation or measurement will you make? Why does the plant have to be kept in the light and watered?
- What will you use as a **control**?

What did you find?

The children in the school 'Go for Green!' club decided to test all the suggestions to improve the health of the plant. They thought that measuring how tall each plant grew would be the best way to measure, as only healthy plants will grow well.

Remedy	Amount plant grew in one week (cm)
no change (control)	3
tomato feed	15
house-plant food	12
new soil	10
new soil and tomato feed	14
new soil and house-plant food	12

- Which plant grew best? Did having new soil in the pot make a difference?

- What conclusion can you make about making a plant grow really well? Which method would you use to help the sick plant?

- Draw a graph of your results. What kind of graph will you choose? Why?

Can you do better?

Was it accurate to say 'use a small amount of food'?

How would you improve the accuracy of the investigation? Why would using a whole tray of plants be a good idea?

Now predict

- The local garden centre is running a competition for children to grow the biggest marrow. You have decided to enter. Part of the competition is to write down exactly what you did to make your marrow so big.

- What instructions would you give? You must be accurate, so the judges can repeat your instructions next year and grow the same-sized marrow.

Identifying living things

Who are you?

'Kangaroo' means 'What is that?' Kangaroo is the word local people told explorers when they asked the name of a strange new animal.

Every known living thing has a name so it can be identified. We use keys to identify and name living things. A key is a series of questions with 'yes' or 'no' answers – "Has it got six legs?" – or questions with optional answers – "How many legs has it got? Are there four, six or eight?" You answer questions until you identify the living thing.

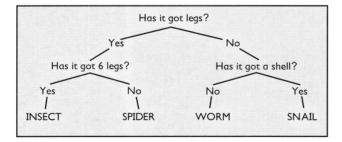

A consumer survey

A food chain shows the eating patterns of animals and plants. In any habitat there will be plants and animals that either provide food or eat it.

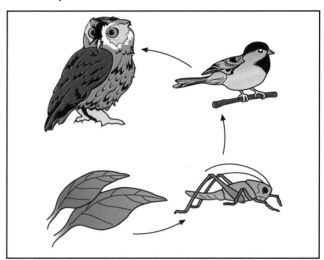

Every food chain starts with a plant. It is called a 'producer'. It uses water and air and the energy of sunlight to manufacture the food that animals eat. It also uses the food to grow itself, so it can produce more food. Animals are called 'consumers' because they eat, or consume, plants or other animals. Some animals are called 'predators', because they eat other animals. The animals they eat are called 'prey'.

Things to do

Are you dependent?

Look at the different habitats around your school. Remember, a habitat provides a home for the plants and animals living there. It will be a safe place as well as a place to rest, eat and bring up young.

- Choose a habitat, such as a hedge, pond or flowerbed. List all the animals and plants you find. Look for a plant that is a producer: then an animal that feeds on the plant; and an animal that feeds on that animal. Is there a plant that gives the animals shelter? How might the plants depend on the animals? Make a list of all you find.

- Now link all the plants and animals together in a food chain. Label the producer and the consumers. Try to label which consumers are predators and which are prey.

These animals are both consumers, but the owl is also a predator

Digging deeper

**Food chains
Food and feeding**

Find out:

- more about food chains.
- what an ecosystem is.

Did you know?

- Green plants are the source of all the oxygen we breathe. Pond and sea plants, including tiny green plankton, produce tonnes of oxygen.

- The Amazon Rainforest alone gives off enough oxygen for half the world's population to live.

I wonder ...

Animals need to hunt or graze for their food. They need to be able to move around. But plants don't move around. Why not? How can they keep still and get the energy they need?

Plants and their roots

Things to learn

- The root anchors the plant in the soil.
- The root takes in water and nutrients.
- Different plants live in different soils.

This plant was grown without soil, but it still needed nutrients

Anchors away!

What part of the plant **anchors** it to stop it being blown away? The roots grip the soil. The roots have other tasks, too. They take in water and nutrients from the soil.

If you protected the plant so that it didn't need to be anchored, then there wouldn't be any need for soil. All the nutrients some plants need can be given in water. Scientists have been growing plants without soil for many years. It is called **hydroponics**. 'Hydro' means water.

All shapes and sizes

Roots come in all shapes and sizes. Some plants have one long thick root growing down into the soil. This is called a 'tap' root. These are the juiciest roots to eat! Carrots and parsnips are tap roots. What other roots do we eat?

Some roots are thinner and longer. They spread out just below the surface of the soil, so they can collect as much as possible of the rainwater that falls. Trees do this. Their roots spread out through the ground as much as their branches do above!

These roots support the tree above the ground

Roots for the job

No matter what shape the root is, or what size, all roots do the same job. What is their job?

- Look at the labels of some plants at a garden centre. Some plants grow well in heavy **waterlogged** or boggy ground and others grow better if the soil is well drained. Others grow in shady conditions. Why is the type of soil important to the plant?

- Draw a table of plants and the conditions they grow best in. Which ones grow in shady conditions? Do these plants grow well in damp or dry ground? What patterns can you spot?

- Look at the roots of plants that grow in boggy ground and those that grow in very dry ground. What differences are there?

Seaweed floats in the water, but has a holdfast to secure it

Digging deeper

**Cells and systems
Plant plumbing**

Find out:

- more about roots and the function they perform.
- what root hair cells are.

Did you know?

- Tall people often have large feet. Tall plants usually have large roots.

- Plants have very tiny hairs on their roots. These are used to take in water and nutrients from the soil.

I wonder ...

Roots are used to take in water and nutrients, and to anchor the plant in the soil. Why does the plant need this anchor?

Life in the soil

Things to learn

- Different types of soil are found in different places.
- Different organisms live in different types of soil.
- You can identify plants and animals using a key.

Snail's pace

What is 'snail's pace'? It is how fast a snail moves across a surface. But what surface will a snail move fastest over?

Snails live in the garden, travelling over the surface of the soil. They leave a 'slime', or mucus trail, so you can see where they've been. This mucus helps them to **glide** over rough or dry surfaces. What sort of soil do you think they will choose to travel on?

I am a mole and I live in a hole

Actually, moles live in long tunnels that they dig themselves. A sure sign that moles have been digging is mounds of soil on the ground. Moles choose soil that is easy to dig through and doesn't collapse on them. They are adapted to living underground. They have claws to dig through the soil, but they have poor **eyesight**. Can you think why?

Scavenger plants

When animals die their bodies decay, providing nutrients to the soil. In the Arctic, the soil is so lacking in these nutrients that plants germinate and flower next to a decaying body, where more nutrients are to be found.

Using a key

A key is a way of identifying something unknown.

- Collect together some vegetables – or some pictures of vegetables. Decide on a yes/no question that divides them into two groups, such as 'is it green?' or 'is it round?' Divide your groups on that basis. Now look at one of the groups and decide on a question that will split it, such as 'is it yellow?' or 'does it grow underground?' Now split the other group, and go on splitting until you get down to individual vegetables. Now you can use your key to identify an 'unknown' vegetable. 'Is it green? No. Is it long? Yes. Does it live above ground? No. Is it orange? Yes. It's a carrot!'

Digging deeper

**Classification
What is classification?**

Find out:

- how scientists group living things together.
- the names of the groups of living things.

Did you know?

- Scientists use a key like this to identify plants and animals they can't name. A book called The British Flora lists every plant growing in Britain. By answering the questions correctly, you can give a name to any plant you find!

I wonder ...

There are plants to be found in almost every type of soil. Why do some plants that grow in poor soil trap and digest flies?

Adapting to a habitat

If you want to beat the rest ...

You've got to adapt. Plants have adapted. They can grow anywhere. Some have adapted to grow in very cold places like the Arctic and very hot, humid places like **tropical rainforests**.

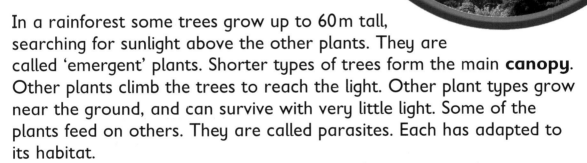

In a rainforest some trees grow up to 60 m tall, searching for sunlight above the other plants. They are called 'emergent' plants. Shorter types of trees form the main **canopy**. Other plants climb the trees to reach the light. Other plant types grow near the ground, and can survive with very little light. Some of the plants feed on others. They are called parasites. Each has adapted to its habitat.

This is a white ptarmigan in winter

Now you see me, now you don't

Any animal that is the prey of another will hide from its predator. This helps it to survive. The fur colour of some mammals is adapted to its habitat. This is called camouflage. Some wild rabbits grow white fur in winter and brown fur in summer. The ptarmigan bird lives in the Arctic and has white feathers in winter. It is camouflaged in the snow and hidden from its predators. But this doesn't stop it from being hunted by the Arctic fox, which also grows a white coat in winter.

Suits you

You will see different types of plants and animals at the beach to those in the fields. Will you find a starfish in a field, or a rabbit on the beach? Do oak trees grow on the beach, or seaweed on land?

Certain animals are ideally suited to living in a rock pool, and others to living in a field. Think of some reasons why you won't find these rock pool creatures living in a field. Think why the bluebells might not grow in a **rock pool**!

- Compare two different habitats, such as a field and the seashore. List all the plants and animals found in each place. Do any live in both? If so, how are they different in each habitat? How are these living things adapted to their environment?

- Invent a creature that is adapted to the habitat of your school classroom.

Digging deeper

> **Adaptation**
> **Life in the ocean**

Find out:

- how organisms that live on the bottom of the ocean feed.
- how they are adapted to their life.

Did you know?

- Some seaweed has small 'bladders', like small balloons, in its fronds. These are filled with air that allow it to float on the surface of the sea. Here it can use sunlight to photosynthesize like other plants.

I wonder ...

The Earth is gradually warming up. This is because of people's actions. It could make the ice at the North and South Poles melt. What will the effect be on the world's sea level?

6A Review

What have you learned?

- Green plants use sunlight to produce food called starch so they can grow.
- Green plants are a source of food as they are at the start of almost every food chain.
- Animals and plants are adapted to their own habitat.
- Different animals and plants live in different habitats.
- Fertilizers are added to soils to provide plants with nutrients for health.
- Plants and animals are in a feeding relationship called a food chain.
- You can use a key to identify plants and animals.

Find out more about ...

Life Processes and Living Things

- Rachel Carson, who worked on protecting the environment.
- how you can help look after your local habitats.

Check-up

The Go for Green club want to grow some tomatoes. They have a shady area in the school grounds. It is on a slope, AND the soil isn't very deep. They are concerned that their plants haven't done very well. Explain what they have done wrong and how they can grow healthy tomatoes.

The answer!

Do you remember the question about fertilizers and pesticides?

When fertilizers get into the rivers, they encourage the growth of river plants. This chokes up the river so it can't flow properly. Fish depend on flowing water for food and oxygen. Without it they die.

A pesticide is a chemical that kills pests on the farmers' crops. If it gets into the river then it may kill organisms there as well.

6B Micro-organisms

- All living things feed, grow and reproduce.
- All living things need nutrients to be healthy.
- All living things have a life cycle to ensure survival.
- Different organisms are found in different habitats.

Do you like yoghurt? Did you know it is made from milk ... that has gone sour! In fact the method is carefully controlled, so it doesn't taste 'off'. The process involves 'bugs' called micro-organisms, or microbes. Microbes are so small we can't see them without a microscope, but for such small creatures they are very important. They help make cheese, wine and bread. Some can be harmful, and make these same foods bad for us to eat. Helpful or harmful, we can't live without them. They are even inside you, helping you digest your food!

Skills check

Can you ...

- measure volume and temperature?
- make careful observations?
- explain what you find out from your science knowledge?

Words to learn

bacteria	mould
bug	pasteurize
germ	sterilize
microbe	virus
micro-organism	yeast

Let's find out ...

Do you eat 'fresh food'? You may think you do, but is it really?
Look at the photo. Which of these items was really fresh? Which were preserved? Can you explain why some food is preserved?

Micro-organisms and you

- Micro-organisms are too small to be seen.
- Some micro-organisms can be harmful.
- We cannot survive without some micro-organisms.

Invisible life

Micro-organisms are too small to see with our naked eyes. Ten of them would fit in the millimetre measure of a ruler, with many of them being much smaller. So how do we know they exist?

When you see mouldy food, you are seeing colonies or groups of microbes. Yoghurt and cheese can only be made from microbes growing in the food.

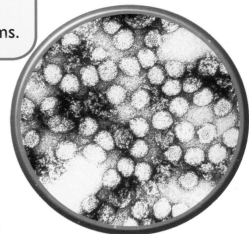

This microbe causes yellow fever

Look out, we're under attack!

Can't we fight them? I could rip them up.

No, lad. They're far too small. We can't see them, but they can harm us.

Sir, sir, help is at hand, the big brush is coming!

Attack!

Your mouth is under attack all the time, from **bacteria**. These bacteria are a type of micro-organism that thrive in the conditions in our mouths. The bacteria turn the sugar from our food into acid, which then attacks our teeth, causing tooth decay. Brushing regularly reduces the number of bacteria.

When you are ill you react to the microbes that are attacking your body. Chicken pox and some kinds of colds and flu are caused by microbes. What do they all have in common? What other names do we use for them?

Athlete's foot is caused by micro-organisms that are a kind of mould, or fungus, related to mushrooms!

How do these diseases spread between people? Does the rhyme 'coughs and sneezes spread diseases' mean anything? Explain why.

Little rotters

If there weren't any microbes to break down and rot dead animals and plant material, then we would be knee-deep in waste. There would be no way of replacing the nutrients in the soil that the plants need to grow and be healthy. There wouldn't be any compost to put on the garden either.

- What sort of objects rot to form **compost**? Collect a variety of objects and see if they decay. Put them outside somewhere safe. Leave your collection of objects for a couple of weeks and then look at them. Which ones have rotted most? Don't handle rotted material!

Biographies

Louis Pasteur
Anton Van Leeuwenhoek

Find out:

- more about how the existence of microbes was discovered.
- who was involved in the discovery of microbes and what they did.
- which microbes they discovered.

Did you know?

- 500 bacteria only cover a full stop!
- This means that you would need 160 000 million bacteria to fill a teaspoon!
- Some bacteria can make stone decay. They produce acid, just like the bacteria in our mouths, but the acid is so strong it rots the stone away.

I wonder ...
If the word 'bacteria' is the plural, then what is the word for a single micro-organism of this kind?

Investigating micro-organisms

Your challenge

- Discover the conditions microbes require to grow well.
- Decide the best way to observe the microbes' growth.
- Explain whether the evidence shows that microbes are living things.

> ⚠ You must **NOT** open the plastic bags once they are sealed with the ties. Microbes can be harmful and can travel through the air.

> I wonder why our light only stays on a short while?

> Have you noticed the air warms up when the light comes on?

> Yeah, I feel like feeding, growing and dividing when it gets warm.

> What we need is to find somewhere warm and moist …

What to do

Class 6JC want to investigate microbes. How will they grow them? What will they observe? Which idea would you use?

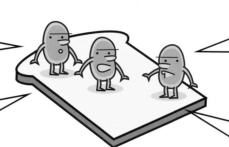

> We will use different types of food to grow the microbes. The food will be put into different plastic bags in the same place.

> We want to use the same type of food in different conditions. This will be dry bread, wet bread, dry toast and wet toast in warm and cold conditions.

What you need

- transparent plastic bags or containers
- ties for the bags
- some bread

What to check

Class 6JC have agreed to count the microbe **colonies** produced after four days. Which bread will produce the most mould? What do they need to keep the same?

Now try it yourselves. What do you think will happen?

What did you find?

Class 6JC produced this table of results from their investigation.

Conditions	Number of colonies
warm and damp	25
warm and dry	10
cold and damp	14
cold and dry	1

Class 6JC can only draw a bar chart of their results. Why?

- Draw a graph of your results. What pattern can you see? Which conditions does this microbe grow best in? What did you notice about the bread with the most colonies on it? Is a microbe a living thing? What evidence in your investigation supports this?

Can you do better?

Class 6JC only had one set of results. This doesn't make the results very reliable. What could you do, when setting up the investigation, to ensure that you really had reliable evidence?

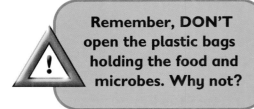

Remember, DON'T open the plastic bags holding the food and microbes. Why not?

Now predict

- Class 6AG are also investigating microbes growing on food. They are trying to prevent their food from producing mould. What conditions would you recommend they keep their food in so that it keeps longer?

Using micro-organisms

Things to learn

- Micro-organisms can be used to make food and drink.
- Micro-organisms can cause food poisoning.
- We use micro-organisms to make us well.

Foods with microbes growing on them.

Edible mould

Mould is a microbe. Would you eat mouldy bread? No. But would you eat blue cheese? You might not eat the bread, but the blue 'veins' in cheese are also mould! The difference is that the cheese has been made so only the right type and amount of mould grows in it. This makes it both safe and tasty to eat.

Meat can have microbes growing on it. It starts to smell 'off' when the microbes are growing. If you ate food that looked like this, it would give you food poisoning. Your body will throw the bad food out of you. You will be very **sick**.

If food is not **preserved**, microbes will feed from it before we do. In what ways do we preserve food? How can we package food to prevent microbes spoiling it? Think about drying, canning, cooking and freezing.

A close-up of microbes

Microbe wars

If you have an infection, the doctor may give you an 'antibiotic', either as a tablet or an injection. This kills the microbe making you ill. The antibiotic may have been made by another microbe! You must take all of the antibiotic or bugs will adapt to resist it. We also use the microbes to make other chemicals that can improve our lives. This is called **'biotechnology'**.

All rise

Yeast is a type of microbe that is used to make some food and drink, like ginger beer and bread. When it is growing well, it produces a gas called carbon dioxide. This can be seen as bubbles in the drinks. It also makes bread rise. If you look, you can see the holes in bread made by the gas bubbles. But in what conditions will it produce the most gas? How will you measure the gas production?

- Put some warm water in a milk bottle. Add some yeast, and some sugar to feed the yeast. Stretch a balloon over the top of the bottle. What happens to the balloon? Can you expain why?

- Now try the same investigation using cold water. What differences do you predict? Try it and see.

Biographies

Alexander Fleming

Find out:

- what important discovery Alexander Fleming made.

- more about how the discovery was made.

Did you know?

- The biotechnology industry is growing so much that it will change our lives completely by the end of this century, just as computers did last century.

- Salting, canning, drying, irradiating, boiling, curing and freezing are all methods of preserving foods.

I wonder ...

Canning kills microbes by heating and driving off air, which deprives them of oxygen. What does freezing and drying do to microbes? How do salting, curing and irradiating work?

6B Review

- Micro-organisms can cause illness.
- They can also cause useful changes and harmful decay.
- Micro-organisms can be used to make certain foods, like yoghurt and bread.
- Micro-organisms are living things and need warm and damp conditions to grow well.
- Food poisoning is caused by micro-organisms growing on food.
- Micro-organisms can be transferred from person to person.

Find out more about ...

Life Processes and Living Things

- how microbes make other foods.
- the immune system and how to fight disease.

Check-up

Class 4MY are about to eat their lunch. They have just been doing some work with minibeasts outside and haven't washed their hands. Explain to them why they should wash their hands before eating their lunch.

Dirty hands!

Yummy!

The answer!

Remember the question about food?

If food is left out, microbes will be able to grow on it, perhaps making the food harnful to eat. However, food preservation changes the condition of food to prevent microbes growing on it. Bacon is usually smoked and then packaged in an airtight container. Jam is preserved by boiling sugar and sealing in an airtight jar. Milk is parsteurized.

6C More about dissolving

- Some solids dissolve in water and some don't.
- Solids that don't dissolve can be separated by filtering.
- A solution is made when a solid dissolves in a liquid.
- When a solid does dissolve it is still in the liquid.
- Temperature is a measure of how hot and cold things are.

Have you ever wondered how Robinson Crusoe survived on a desert island all that time? He found a fresh water spring. Without it, he would have had to know about dissolving and evaporating. He was surrounded by sea — water with salt dissolved in it. But he needed pure water to drink. How could he get pure water? How could he use the same processes and produce seasoning for his food too?

Skills check

Can you …

- measure temperature with a thermometer?
- draw a clear graph?
- measure the volume of a liquid?

Words to learn

accurate	evaporate	solution
average	insoluble	temperature
condense	mixture	thermometer
decant	pure	
dissolve	saturated	

Let's find out …

If you are making an instant soup do you put the water or the powder in the cup first? What happens to the soup powder? What temperature of water do you start with? How can you make the drink faster? Before you drink the soup you have to leave it for a few minutes. Why? Some soups have added croutons or vegetables. Why don't they disappear when the water is added?

contents of one sach…
…or mug, add ⅓ pint (190 ml) …
…ng water and stir well.

INGREDIENTS: DRIED GLUCOSE SYRUP, MODIFIED STARCH, DRIED SWEETCORN, VEGETABLE FAT, SALT, FLAVOUR ENHANCERS: MONOSODIUM GLUTAMATE, SODIUM '5' RIBONUCLEOTIDES; DRIED CHICKEN, HYDROLYSED VEGETABLE PROTEIN, FLAVOURINGS, CASEINATE, DRIED ONION, DRIED TOMATO, ACIDITY REGULATOR: E340, EMULSIFIERS: E471, E472(b): STABILISER: E412: HERBS, COLOUR: E160(b), SPICES, ANTIOXIDANT: E320

31 gram **1.1** oz per twin pack

Filtering and sieving

Things to learn

- Some solids don't dissolve in water.
- These insoluble solids can be separated.
- Filtering is similar to sieving.

Now you see it ...

When you put some solids in water, they sink to the bottom or float on the top. They don't dissolve. These are insoluble solids.

If you want to get the clean water back, you can separate the solid from the liquid. There is more than one way to do this.

If the solid sinks, you can pour the liquid off the top. This is called **decanting**.

If the solid is suspended in the water you can sieve or filter it.

Separate ways

How many ways can you separate a solid from a liquid? A sieve works by holding the large solid pieces in the sieve so the water can escape through the holes. But can you separate fine sand and water using a sieve? Why not? What would you use?

A filter will remove insoluble solids from liquids

Water, water…

You're stranded on a desert island. The Sun's rays are beating down. You are desperate for some shade and a drink. You've been there three hours and there's no sign of rescue. All you have is a first aid kit and some plastic cups. There isn't any clean water on the island, and you've heard stories of people going mad if they drink seawater. What are you going to do?

- Use the plastic cup and anything that is in the first aid kit and on the beach to produce clean water from the muddy puddle. Why would it be better to use the muddy puddle water than the seawater? Think carefully about all you've learnt about separating insoluble solids from a liquid.

Digging deeper

> **Separating materials**
> **Sieves and filters**

Find out:

- what an air cleaner in a car engine does.
- how a filter is like a sieve.

Did you know?

- You have filters – in your nose! These are little hairs that trap large particles of dust that you breathe in. There is also sticky mucus in your nose that traps the smaller particles. This stops them getting to your lungs, and making you cough.

- Fish have filters in their gills.

I wonder …

If you look closely at a tea bag what can you see? How does the tea inside dissolve?

Separating solids and liquids

Things to learn

- A solution is a solid dissolved in a liquid.
- The dissolved solid can't be removed from a solution by filtering.
- When the water evaporates from a solution, the solid is left.

What's the answer?

The answer to a problem is also the solution to it. Is this the type of solution you expect to see here – lots of answers? What is the other type of solution? Some solids 'disappear' when you put them in water.

The solid hasn't really disappeared. It has dissolved to form a solution. Everywhere you look in the solution you will find some of the solid. Some solutions are colourless, some are coloured. They can all be transparent. As long as they are not too thick the light will pass through them.

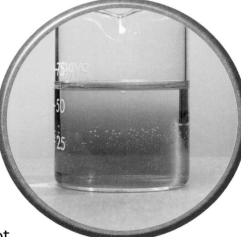

Ink is a solution of coloured pigment in water

Which to remove?

How do you get the solid in a solution out again? Because the solid is dissolved in the liquid, it can't be sieved. The particles are too mixed up and too small. Would a filter work? Try it and see.

To get the dissolved particles of solid back, you may need to remove the water. What do you know about making liquid water evaporate?

Remember what happens to a puddle on a warm day? It eventually dries up. The water doesn't disappear though. It evaporates and turns from a liquid into water vapour that escapes into the air.

Filtering removes insoluble solids from muddy water

Going, going, gone

If you leave a solution in a warm place the water will evaporate leaving the dissolved solid in the bottom of the dish. Instead of removing the solid from the liquid you are removing the water from the solid.

- Place some different solutions in dishes in a warm place. How much solution should you use? What do you have to keep the same for each solution to make this a fair test? What will happen? How long should you leave it? Where does the liquid go?

You can collect the salt from sea water by evaporation

Exploring

Separating mixtures
Separating a solution

Find out:

- more about how to separate a dissolved solid from the liquid it is dissolved in.
- what the difference is between a solute and a solvent.
- what happens when a solid dissolves.

Did you know?

- When a liquid evaporates, it cools a surface. Sweat evaporating cools your skin.
- When you put nail varnish on it is wet. If you leave it for a couple of minutes it dries. This is because the solvent containing the varnish evaporates, leaving a hard, shiny layer on your nails.

I wonder ...

Would evaporation be the best way to separate rice from water? Explain what you would do.

Making pure water

Things to learn

- When a solution evaporates, the water becomes pure.
- Only the water evaporates from a solution.

Where does it go?

What happens to the liquid when you leave a solution in a warm place? What is left in the bottom of the dish?

If you want to recover the solid that was dissolved in the water, then you leave the solution in a warm place. The water evaporates, leaving the solid behind. But where does the water go? Does some of the solid leave the dish with the water or is the condensed water pure?

Solid particles are bigger than liquid ones. The solid is too heavy to escape from the solution, so the liquid is the only part that escapes. The water may condense on a cold surface to form pure water.

You get pure water when you evaporate and condense a salt solution. Do you get clear water if you do the same with inky water?

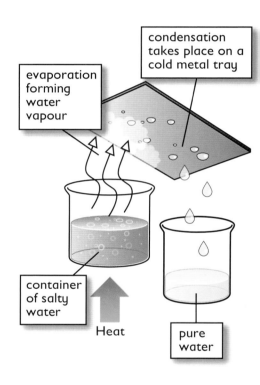

condensation takes place on a cold metal tray

evaporation forming water vapour

container of salty water

Heat

pure water

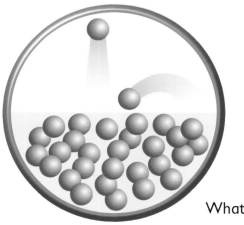

Energy

If you have more food, you have more energy so you can run around more. A particle needs energy, too. If you give it heat energy it will move faster. If a liquid particle moves faster it can sometimes escape from the liquid. Liquid particles that escape become gas particles.

What process is this?

... not a drop to drink

Remember your island? You solved the problem of getting water from the dirty puddle, but now the water has nearly all gone and only sea water remains. Give two reasons why the water in the puddle has gone?

You've still not seen any sign of rescue. The Sun's rays are beating down just as hard. You need to have water to drink. You can only survive for a couple of days without it.

Whilst you've been on the island, you have found plenty of useful items, either naturally or washed up by the tide. What would you use to collect pure water to drink?

- Make a plan to get pure water. Draw and label a picture of what you would do.

Exploring

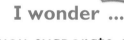

Changing materials
Heating up

Find out:
- how the particles of liquid evaporate from a solution.

Did you know?

- Evaporation and condensation are part of the natural water cycle. Water evaporates from the sea, and rises into the air. As it rises, it cools and condenses. This turns it into water droplets and clouds. These cool further, grow bigger and fall as rain. This is called the water cycle or the rain cycle.

I wonder ...

If you evaporate cola, will you get pure water? What will be left in the bottom of the container?

Dissolving jelly

- Discover how to dissolve jelly fast.
- Make a prediction based on your scientific understanding.
- Draw a line graph and explain what it shows.

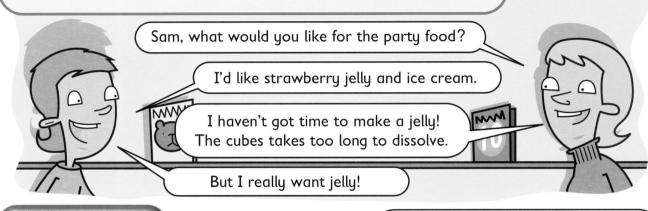

Sam, what would you like for the party food?

I'd like strawberry jelly and ice cream.

I haven't got time to make a jelly! The cubes takes too long to dissolve.

But I really want jelly!

What to do

At school Sam tells her classmates about the problem with the jelly. They carry out an investigation with jelly, to find how to make it dissolve in water more quickly. Which idea would you use? Would you use any of them? What do you think will happen in each of these investigations?

Let's see how hot the water needs to be to dissolve the jelly quickly.

What about cutting the jelly into smaller pieces and seeing which dissolves fastest?

We could try stirring the water.

We could time how long the jelly takes to dissolve in water.

What you need

- thermometers
- some jelly
- a pair of scissors
- several containers
- a stopwatch
- spoons

What to check

Now try it yourselves.

- The class decided to change the water temperature and time how long the jelly took to dissolve.
- What will they have to keep the same?

What did you find?

The children produced this set of results.

Temperature of water (°C)	Time for jelly to dissolve (minutes)
10	20
20	14
30	8
40	2
50	1

- These results show a **trend**. What is it? If you draw a graph of the results, what type of graph would you draw? What does it show?

- Does the trend shown in the graph match what you thought would happen?

- What do you think would happen if an adult safely used boiling water at 100 °C?

Do not use water hotter than hot tap water!

Can you do better?

The group only had time to do the investigation once. What advice would you give them about doing the investigation again? Why should they try repeating it?

Why would making the pieces of jelly smaller make a difference to how long it takes to dissolve? Would stirring make a difference?

Now predict

- If you were late for school and you wanted sugar in your tea, how would you make it dissolve fast enough for you to drink it before you had to go?

Dissolving sugar

- Discover how sweet you can make your tea.
- Produce a line graph of results and explain what it shows.
- Explain why you need to repeat measurements.

How many sugars do you have in your tea?

Just one, please.

I have twelve in my tea!

Don't you leave some sugar in the bottom of the cup?

It depends how much tea I have.

What to do

One of the children has a very sweet tooth, but will 12 teaspoons of sugar dissolve in a cup of tea? The children decide to test out their idea, using a teaspoon and some warm water, so they can see when the sugar has dissolved. They have a few ideas about what will happen and why. Which do you agree with, or do you have your own idea?

 The sugar will dissolve in the water until the water can't hold any more.

 The more water you use the more sugar will dissolve.

When the water won't hold any more sugar, it will lie at the bottom of the cup.

 Maybe if you add the sugar slowly then the water can dissolve more.

What you need

- some sugar
- a measuring cylinder
- a teaspoon

What to check

Now try it yourselves.

- The children decided to stir the water as they added sugar and to keep adding sugar until they could see it on the bottom of the cup.
- What else must be kept the same?

What did you find?

The children found out how many teaspoons of sugar dissolved in one cup of water. They then tried different sized cups to see if their other idea was true, that if there is more water then more sugar can be dissolved in it.

- How did the children measure the volume of the water? What kind of graph can be drawn from these results? Draw one for yourself. What pattern can you see in the graph?
- Is there a limit to the number of teaspoons of sugar that water can hold?

Volume of water (ml)	Number of teaspoons of sugar
10	2
15	3
20	4
30	6
55	11

Can you do better?

The children only used one kind of sugar. Could using different sugar make a difference?

Now predict

- If you had a cup that could hold 80 ml of water, how many teaspoonfuls of sugar would you expect to dissolve?
- How would the temperature of the water make a difference to the results?

Mixing solids and liquids

- A solution is saturated when no more solid will dissolve.
- Water can dissolve more of some solids than others.

Can't take any more

When a piece of fabric is saturated it is holding as much water as it can. Your clothes might get saturated with water when you are out in a rainstorm. But water itself can be 'saturated'. When a solid is added to water and dissolves, the solid particles are mixing with the liquid particles. Eventually the liquid particles don't have any space to hold any more solid particles, so no more will dissolve. This is called a 'saturated solution'.

If you have a full cup of tea and you add two teaspoons of sugar, what happens? Does the cup overflow? Try it. What does this show about the sugar and the water particles?

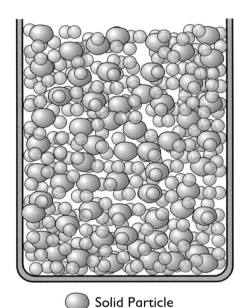

⬤ Solid Particle
◯ Water Particle

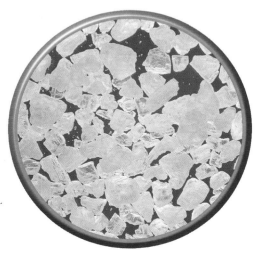

These are crystals
or grains

Does grain size matter?

Look at the size of grains or crystals of sugar and salt. Use the microscope. What do they look like? Look at some of the other substances that you know dissolve in water. Are the grain sizes all the same? Is there a link between grain size and how much will dissolve in water? What is it?

If you had to carry some large objects and some small ones, which could you carry more of? How is this a picture of what happens in water?

Things to do

That's the limit

Is there a limit to how much different solids will dissolve in water? Is the limit the same for all solids? For example, can the same volume of water dissolve two teaspoons of salt, or two teaspoons of sugar, or two teaspoons of cocoa powder?

- Plan an investigation to find out the answer to this question. What will you have to keep the same to ensure a fair test?

- How will you get accurate results?

- Plan the investigation to get results that can be presented as a line graph.

Digging deeper

Separating materials
Solutions

Find out:

- more about different types of solutions made with solids or liquids in water.

- what a miscible solution is.

There is oil on the water from this crashed tanker – oil and water are not 'miscible'

Did you know?

- Salad dressings are made of oil and vinegar. They don't mix very well. If you add mustard to flavour the dressing, the oil and vinegar will mix better. The mustard acts as a kind of 'glue'.

I wonder ...

Flour has very tiny grains, but it doesn't dissolve. What happens when you put it into water? Why?

6C Review

- Insoluble solids can be separated from liquids by filtering.
- A solution is a solid dissolved in a liquid.
- When the water evaporates from a solution, the solid is left and the water collected is pure.
- A solution is saturated when no more solid will dissolve in the liquid.
- Water can dissolve more of some solids than others.

Find out more about ....

Materials and their Properties

- uses of evaporation and condensation in industry.
- what happens to the particles when a solid dissolves.

Check-up

John is making his mother a cup of coffee with sugar. He puts cold water into the cup, then instant coffee. He can't get the water to go coffee coloured. When he pours out the water he finds brown **sludge** in the bottom of the cup with white grains in it. What has John done wrong in making the coffee? What is the 'sludge' in the bottom of the cup?

The answer!

Remember the question about soup?

When you add boiling water to the soup mix, the powder dissolves to form the 'soup'. The vegetables and croutons are less soluble, and so form the chunks in the soup. If you stir the soup or use hotter water the powder will dissolve faster. You can tell if you haven't added enough water, because the soup is too thick, and not all the powder dissolves.

6D Reversible and irreversible changes

What do you know?

- How to recognize evaporation, condensation, melting, freezing and dissolving.
- That evaporation, condensation, melting, freezing and dissolving are all reversible.
- What happens when materials evaporate, condense, melt, freeze and dissolve.

We are surrounded by many different kinds of materials. Some, like rocks and wood, are natural. But many have been made to do a particular task. To make a new material, other materials have to be changed. Some of these changes may be reversible – we can always go back to where we started. But many are irreversible – a new material is formed, nothing like the old ones!

Skills check

Can you ...

- make careful observations and measurements?
- collect evidence and see how good it is?
- use your evidence to explain what you've found out?
- use your evidence to predict something you don't yet know?

Words to learn

chemical reaction
irreversible
reaction
reversible

Let's find out ...

After the bonfire party, Hardip went round the garden. He collected all the fireworks he had watched the night before. "I'm going to have another firework display tonight," he told his mother. "Not with those fireworks!" said his mother. "Why not?" asked Hardip.

Evaporation

- What happens when solids are added to water.
- How to get an undissolved solid back from water.
- How to get a dissolved solid back from water.
- What happens to some materials as they are heated and cooled.
- Burning materials can be dangerous.

Sand and salt

"It's a disaster," said Mrs Pearson. "The bags have burst, and sand and salt are all mixed together."

"Don't worry, Miss," said Alan. "I know how to separate them." "How can you do that?" his teacher asked. "All you need to know is that salt dissolves – and sand doesn't," said Alan.

Alan used evaporation to get the salt back. He used **filtration** to get the sand back. But which did he do first – and why?

Chocolate eggs

Easter eggs are made from chocolate. To make the shape of the egg, the chocolate is warmed and melted and put in an egg-shaped mould. When it has cooled and hardened, the mould is taken away and the chocolate egg is left. What processes do the egg-makers use? Why is it important that they are reversible? Just think what would happen if the chocolate didn't harden!

What happens with water?

When you add familiar foods to water, such as sugar to your tea, or salt to your soup, you expect them to dissolve. They seem to have disappeared – but you know by the taste that they are still there.

- But what about other safe materials? Does powder paint dissolve easily? Try adding water to **cornflour**, stirring all the time. Try some **indigestion powders** – like 'liver salts'. What happens?

- Finally, try **plaster of Paris**. Something amazing happens! Not all materials need to be heated to speed up dissolving …

Bonfire!

What's left after a bonfire? Some things aren't changed much. You might find nails and screws in the ashes but what about wood? The ashes can't be used to make another wooden box! The change is irreversible.

You can be changed by heat too, but not for the better! Skin can burn easily, so always be careful with fire. If you are ever burned, it is important to take the heat out of the situation. Quickly put your **burnt** fingers or arm under a cold water tap – and keep it there. Without the heat, your skin can recover.

Exploring

Changing materials Burning

Find out:
- more about burning.

Did you know?

- Cooking is the most common way to make irreversible changes. You can't get the eggs and flour back from a cake mixture!

- Rusting is an irreversible change.

I wonder …

What is it that burns when we light a candle? Where does the candle material go – and why can't we burn the candle again?

Making new materials

Your challenge

- Explore what happens when different materials are mixed together.
- Decide whether the changes are reversible.
- Describe new materials that are made.
- Explain what happened, using what you know about science.

James was making a plaster of Paris model. "This feels warm!" he said to his older brother. "What did you do to it?" asked Will. "Did you put it in the oven?" "I didn't do anything to it," said James. "I just mixed the white powder with water."

James was baffled. But Will told him that while lots of changes needed heat, some made heat. Maybe this was one of them. "Try mixing these," Will said, giving him some more kitchen materials. "Don't worry – they're all safe!"

What to do

Mix together some of these:

- plaster of Paris and water
- liver salts and water
- bicarbonate of soda (or baking powder) and vinegar
- washing soda and lemon juice
- cement and water

DO NOT touch soda crystals, cement powder or wet cement. Wash your hands after these activities. **DO NOT** taste any of these materials or solutions.

What you need

- materials to mix
- water
- a measuring cylinder

What to check

Now try it yourselves.

- Use small amounts of these materials.
- Observe carefully what happens.
- Record what happens and think about what you already know.

What did you find?

James was surprised with his results. But he was too excited to complete the table properly! He's left some gaps.

Solid to mix	Liquid to mix	What happened	Why I think it happened
plaster of Paris	water	It got warm! The plaster dried out and became hard. This is irreversible.	This is called a reaction. Some reactions need heat to get them going – but some produce heat.
liver salts		It bubbled and fizzed. The liquid was clear but the salts were still there	The salts dissolved in the water. The reaction made a gas. The gas made the liquid bubble.
bicarbonate of soda	vinegar		The reaction made a gas. The gas made the bubbles.
washing soda	lemon juice	Lots of fizzing.	
cement		It got a bit warm as the cement powder mixed with the water. It hardened after a while.	This is another reaction that produced heat. No way will I get the cement powder back.

- Copy and complete the table using your own test results.

James showed Will his results. "These are all **chemical reactions**," his brother told him.

Can you get an irreversible change without mixing chemicals?

Let me saw your leg off and I'll tell you!

Can you do better?

How good is your evidence? Can you make any general rules about your results?

How do we use these reactions to help us in everyday life? When do builders, or cooks, or people with indigestion, use these new materials?

Now predict

- James melted butter. Then he melted chocolate. He planned to make chocolate crispy cakes. "Are those irreversible reactions?" asked his big brother.

Irreversible change

Your challenge

- Find out what happens when different materials are burned.
- Discover what new materials are made.
- Recognize that some of these new materials cannot be seen.
- Take every possible precaution when burning materials.

Follow your teacher's safety advice. Tie back long hair. Do not lean across a burning candle, or carry it around.

"Where does the candle wax go, Dad?"
"I don't know," said Andrea's dad.
"Maybe it just disappears."

Andrea knew that couldn't be right.
"I think something new is made," said Andrea.
"But we can't see it."

What to do

Andrea puzzled about the disappearing candle. "I think the candle must make a gas of some kind," she thought. "Only a gas could be invisible."

What would you do?

Suppose one of the gases was water. How can you tell that there is water in the air?

Maybe things just burn away to nothing.

That can't be right. When things burn, new things are made.

I think candles burn to give us a gas – or maybe some gases.

If we can't see them, how can we tell they are there?

What you need

- a burning candle, secured in a safe tray of sand
- a tin tray or can lid held in pliers or tongs
- a glass jar of ice

What to check

Now try it yourselves.

- What do you think will happen?
- How will you test for the gases?
- Will you be able to name any?

What did you find?

Andrea watched as the candle burned down. Here are her observations.

1. The candle is white and cold. It is a solid. When we light it, the **wick** turns black. The solid candle becomes liquid near the wick. The flame is blue near the wick, then yellow further away. You can smell the burning.

2. We held a tin lid above the flame. It got smoky with **soot**. We think that might be from the wick. We held a cold glass jar above the flame. Water condensed on the jar. It dripped onto the candle. So one new material was water.

3. Our teacher told us that candles produce carbon dioxide gas, too.

- Was Andrea correct in saying the candle makes a gas when it burns?

- How could you test for carbon dioxide?

Can you do better?

Andrea held tiny pieces of different safe materials in the flame using the tongs. She was curious to see what was made when they were burned. She recorded her observations in a table. You could do the same.

Now predict

- When Andrea cooked breakfast, she always burnt the toast. What's the difference between heating things and burning things, she wondered?

6D Review

What have you learned?

- You know what happens when solids are added to water.
- You know how to get an undissolved solid back from water.
- You know how to get a dissolved solid back from water.
- You know what happens to some materials as they are heated and cooled.
- You know that burning materials can be dangerous.
- You know what happens when different materials are mixed together.
- You can decide whether changes are reversible.
- You know how to describe new materials that are made.
- You know what happens when different materials are burned and what new materials are made.
- You know that some new materials cannot be seen.
- You know to take every possible precaution when burning materials.
- You know how to make careful observations and measurements.
- You can collect evidence and see how good it is.
- You can use your evidence to explain what you've found out.
- You can use your evidence to predict something you don't yet know.

Find out more about ...

Materials and their Properties

- how new materials, like **ceramics**, are made in industry.

Check-up

Sharon and John have a gas barbecue. "It's great," they said. "The gas just doesn't seem to get used up." Why aren't they right? What is happening to the gas?

The answer!

Hardip couldn't reuse the fireworks as they had been burned and changed irreversibly. The materials in the fireworks had changed to gases, but at least the burning gases had given Hardip a great firework display!

6E Forces in action

What do you know?

- Forces are pushes and pulls.
- Forces act in particular directions.
- We can't see forces but we can measure them and observe what they do.
- Forces can make objects move, stop, change speed, direction or even shape.
- Friction is a force that slows things down.
- Lubrication reduces friction between solid surfaces.
- Air resistance is a force that slows things moving in air.
- Water resistance is a force that slows things moving in water.
- Streamlined shapes can reduce air and water resistance.

Did you know that forces are acting on you all the time? Whenever you do something you are exerting a force. When you take a step, you push against the ground; the ground is also pushing back at you.

Skills check

Can you …

- make careful observations and measurements?
- collect evidence and see how good it is?
- notice patterns in your results?
- explain what you've found out?
- predict something you don't yet know?

Words to learn

action	reaction
forcemeter	upthrust
gravity	weight
newton	

Let's find out …

Mum went to the market. She bought eggs, potatoes and apples and put them into a plastic carrier bag. As she lifted the bag the handles snapped and the groceries fell all over the road. The apples and potatoes rolled down the hill and the eggs broke. Explain why all this happened – as forces in action!

Weight and gravity

Things to learn

- The Earth and all objects are pulled towards each other.
- Gravitational attraction causes objects to have weight.
- Weight is a force.
- Forces are measured in newtons (N).

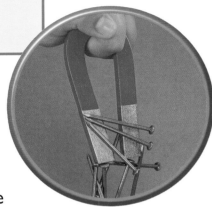

We're all attractive

Gravity is the force that keeps your feet on the ground and the atmosphere in place. If there was no gravity everything, including the air we breathe, would fly off into space.

Every object pulls every other object towards it because of the force of gravity. The force between objects is so tiny we don't notice it compared with the force of Earth's gravity, which pulls everything towards its centre.

Both gravity and magnetism can work over a distance.

Gravity keeps the Moon in orbit around the Earth

Weigh it up

The size of the force of gravity depends on the object's mass (the amount of matter it contains) and its distance from the object it's attracting. Gravity pulls down on everything – solids, liquids or gases – and gives them a force called weight. An object with a small amount of mass has a small weight; an object with a large amount of mass has a large weight. Weight is the force that makes things feel heavy or light.

Walking on the Moon

We can change the weight of an object by reducing its mass (making it lighter), or by adding to its mass (making it heavier), or by moving it away from the Earth and into space (reducing the force of gravity).

Because the Moon is smaller than the Earth it has a smaller force of gravity. Gravity on the Moon is one sixth that of gravity on Earth.

Measure a force

We measure forces in newtons. The symbol for a newton is N. One newton is about the force you would need to pick up an average-sized apple. Ten newtons are roughly the force you would need to lift 1 kg.

A forcemeter measures force. Hook an object onto the spring. Gravity pulls down the object. The force of the pull of gravity on the object stretches the spring and the force in newtons can be read on the scale.

- Try this yourself. Measure the weight in newtons of some objects using a forcemeter.

- Now find the mass of your objects by putting them on a digital balance. Remember, mass is a measure of how much matter something has — we measure mass in grams and kilograms.

- Can you find a connection between mass and weight?

Digging deeper

Forces
Weights and measures

Find out:

- more about how weight can change.
- how to get instant weight loss on another planet!

Did you know?

- On Mars your weight would be three times less than it is on Earth because **Mars** has a weaker gravitational pull.

- If you could stand on **Jupiter** you'd weigh three times as much as you do on Earth because Jupiter's gravity is stronger than Earth's.

I wonder ...

Why is it easier to push a car than a bus?

Direction of forces

Things to learn

- Several forces may act on an object at the same time.
- Forces have strength and direction.
- We represent forces with arrows.

Pair up

Forces don't act alone. When you make a force by pushing or pulling an object, the object pushes or pulls back with an equal force.

When you pull a chair from under a table you use force to move it but you can also feel its equal force pulling back at you. If the chair didn't have an equal force to the force you use to move it, it would be really easy to move.

Try this with an elastic band – if you stretch it you can feel it pulling back at you.

Equal and opposite

If you make a force there will always be an equal force pushing back at you. Your force is called the action and the opposite force is the reaction. The action and reaction are always the same strength but they act in opposite directions. When you run, your feet push down on the ground – that's the action. At the same time, the ground pushes back with the same force but in the opposite direction, up at you – that's the reaction. Try and identify the action and reaction forces of some of your movements.

Off balance

When something is still we say that the forces acting on it are balanced.

The girl in the chair isn't moving because her force on the chair, her weight, is balanced by the push back from the chair. If these forces weren't in balance, she'd fall through the chair!

Things to do

Drawing forces

When we draw forces we need to show the size of the force (how strong a push or pull it is) and also its direction (the way it pushes or pulls). We draw forces as arrows. The length of the arrow shows how strong it is; a short arrow is a weak force, a long arrow is a strong force. The way the arrow points shows the direction of the force. The arrow always points in the direction of movement, whether it's a pull or a push.

Issac Newton first explained gravity

- Draw the force arrows on the pictures on the worksheet.

Biographies

Sir Isaac Newton

Find out:

- about the life and discoveries of Sir Isaac Newton.

Did you know?

- Helicopters, hawks or hornets can hover because the uplift force of their rotors or wings is exactly balanced by the downward pull of gravity.

- To escape the force of the Earth's gravity a rocket needs to accelerate quickly after its launch. The **escape velocity** is about 40 000 km per hour.

I wonder ...

Why is it easier for two people to lift a heavy object than it is for one person to lift it on their own?

Investigating upthrust

- Find out about the upward force water exerts on a submerged object.
- Make careful measurements of force using a forcemeter.
- Use tables to present results and identify patterns within them.

The baby's due in a few weeks! I'm too heavy to go to the gym so I go to aqua aerobic classes instead.

Aqua aerobics? What's that?

Aqua Aerobics

Exercises in a swimming pool. The water supports your weight so it's easier to move.

Philippa decided to find out why it was easier to exercise in water.

What to do

Philippa measured the weight of some objects in newtons. Next she estimated what they would weigh in water. She submerged the objects in water and carefully read the value on her forcemeter.

By taking the weight in water away from the weight in air, Philippa could calculate how much force or **upthrust** the water was pushing with.

What you need

- a forcemeter
- several objects that will sink in water and can be attached to the forcemeter
- a deep bowl of water
- paper towels

What to check

Now try it yourselves.

- How will you make sure that the object does not touch the bottom of the bowl?
- Make sure the forcemeter pointer is at rest
- Repeat the measurement several times to be certain.

What did you find?

Phillipa put the results of her test into a table:

Object	Weight in air (N)	Weight in water (N)	Upthrust of water (N)
staple gun	1	1·5	0·5
bunch of keys	2	0·85	0·15
scissors	0·75	0·55	0·2
corkscrew	3·5	2·8	1·2
hole punch	1·3	0·9	0·4
bags of marbles	1·5	1·1	0·4

Phillipa noticed that the objects always weighed less in water than in air.

She thought that the water was pushing up against the object and supporting some of its weight.

- Draw a table of your results.

Can you do better?

If you did this investigation again is there anything you would change or do differently?

How good is your evidence?

Can you make a general rule about your results?

Now predict

- What do you think is happening to the mass of your objects when they are put into water? If an object had a mass of 200 g in air, what do you think its mass would be when in water? How could you test this?

- Does gravity work through water? How do you know?

Stretching elastic bands

Your challenge

- Find the relationship between an elastic band stretching and the forces acting on it.
- Make careful measurements of length.
- Represent data in a line graph and use this to identify patterns in the data.

Mrs Blair's class is investigating what happens to an elastic band when masses are suspended from it.

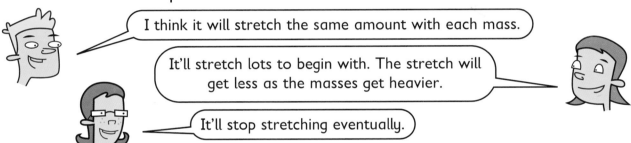

I think it will stretch the same amount with each mass.

It'll stretch lots to begin with. The stretch will get less as the masses get heavier.

It'll stop stretching eventually.

Do you agree with the children? What do you think will happen? Try it yourself.

What to do

Decide what measurement to make. Now add your masses one at a time and record how far the band stretches.

It might be easier if we measured from the table to the bottom of the mass.

Maybe we could mark the length on a piece of card then measure it later.

What you need

- a forcemeter
- a secure hook or pole to attach your forcemeter to
- elastic bands
- hanging masses
- a metre rule

What to check

Now try it yourselves.

- Decide where to measure from.
- Increase the mass by the same amount each time
- Avoid snapping the elastic band.
- Does it matter what sort of elastic band you use
- Record measurements in a table.

What did you find?

Mrs Blair's class all did the same investigation and used the same length and thickness of elastic band. They added 50 g weights and each time they measured the length of the band from top to bottom. They put all of their results together and took a class average. Why do you think they did this?

Total mass added (g)	Length of elastic band (cm)	Length of stretch from resting position (cm)
0	17	0
50	17·5	0·5
100	18·5	1·5
150	19·5	2·5
200	21	4
250	22	5
300	22·5	5·5
350	23	6
400	23	6

They recorded their results in a table.

The class also used a spreadsheet to record their results and drew a line graph using their data. They thought they noticed a pattern in the results.

- Can you see what the pattern is?
- Draw a graph of your results.
  Tell the story of your graph.

Can you do better?

If you did this investigation again would you do anything differently? Why?

Can you write a general rule to explain what was happening?

Could you use your graph to predict how far the elastic band stretches at weights you haven't tried yet?

Would your rule apply to all types of elastic band?

Now predict

- When people do a bungee jump, they throw themselves from a high place attached to a thick elastic cord. The cord bounces back before they hit the ground. Each person must be weighed before they jump. Why is this?

Air resistance

Things to learn

- Air resistance is a force that can slow down a moving object.
- Air resistance acts in the opposite direction to the weight as an object falls.
- Objects with large surface areas have more air resistance than objects with smaller surface areas.

Air friction

Friction is the force that slows down moving objects. It happens when two things rub together. We can overcome friction between moving parts in machinery by using **lubricating oil** or grease. When something moves through air, it rubs against the particles of air, causing friction (air resistance). The faster an object is moving, the greater the friction and the greater the air resistance.

Geronimo!

When **parachutists** jump, gravity pulls them towards the Earth. They open their parachutes to increase their air resistance and slow their descent.

Shape affects air resistance. If an object has a large, flat front surface then the air resistance will be high. Small, pointed front surfaces allow the air to move more quickly over them.

Falling fast

An Italian scientist called Galileo believed that if you dropped two objects of different weights from the same height, and there was zero air resistance, they would reach the ground at the same time because the force of gravity pulls everything equally. It wasn't until **astronauts** did this experiment on the Moon that Galileo was proved right. There was no air on the Moon to resist the pull of its gravity.

Make a parachute

- Make some different-sized parachutes out of tissue paper and thread. Use paperclips to represent a person. Drop your parachutes from the highest safe place you can (the top of a safe stairwell, for instance) and time their **descent** using a stopwatch. What must you do to keep your test fair? Which takes the longest? Which is the fastest? Is it the shape that matters or the surface area? Can you think of some more 'parachute questions' to investigate?

Find the fastest

- Objects meet resistance when they move through water as well as through air. Look for pictures of racing yachts and powerboats. Look at their shape. Think about the forces that make a boat move through water.

Digging deeper

Forces
Action and reaction

Find out:

- more about forces that act on aeroplanes in flight.

Did you know?

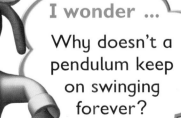

- The fastest aircraft is the Lockheed SR-71. It can reach speeds of over 3500 km per hour.

- Objects that travel through the air very fast get very hot on the outside because of friction. The outside of a space shuttle reaches over 1000 °C as it re-enters the atmosphere.

I wonder ...

Why doesn't a pendulum keep on swinging forever?

Investigating spinners

- Find out how air resistance acts in the opposite direction to the weight of a falling object.
- Calculate surface area.
- Make careful measurements and repeat them.
- Make and interpret a line graph.

I wonder whether spinners behave in the same way as parachutes?

Do big spinners fall slower than small ones?

What about the weight of the spinner?

Or the material it's made from?

What to do

Carry out a fair test to see whether the surface area of the **rotors** affects the speed that the spinner falls.

Make several spinners with different-sized rotors. Add a paper clip at the bottom to steady your spinner and to act as the **load**.

Drop the spinners and time how long they take to reach the ground. Repeat two or three times with each spinner and take an average of your results.

What you need

- spinners with different-sized rotor blades
- paper clips
- stopwatches

What to check

Now try it yourselves.

- How will you keep your test fair?
- Will increasing the size of the rotors change more than one factor?

What did you find?

The children made several measurements using spinners with different-sized wings. Here are their results:

Total wing size (cm^2)	Time taken to reach floor (sec)
112	2·0
91	1·5
70	1·2
49	1·0
28	0·9

The children found that the spinners with the biggest wings fell the slowest. They thought that this was because by increasing the surface area of the spinner, they increased the air resistance. This slowed down the spinner as it moved. Do you agree?

- Use a computer program to plot your results on a graph. Can you find **a line of best fit?**

- Do any of your results look strange? Can you explain your results?

Can you do better?

If you did this investigation again, would you do anything differently? How good is the children's evidence? Did they change anything else when they changed the wing size?

Now predict

- Although the children calculated the wing size in cm^2 they only made their wings longer. Would the results be different if they changed the shape of the rotor? What would happen if the surface area stayed the same but the rotors were fatter rather than longer? Why do you think it would make a difference?

6E Review

- We measure forces in newtons (N).
- You know forces act in pairs.
- You know several forces may act on an object at the same time.
- You know when an object is stationary or moving at a constant speed the forces acting on it are balanced.
- You know gravity is a force that pulls everything to the centre of the Earth.
- We represent forces with arrows.
- You know friction is a force that slows things down.
- You know when an object falls air resistance acts in the opposite direction to the weight.
- You know streamlined shapes can reduce air and water resistance.
- You know water provides an upthrust on objects submerged in water.

Find out more about ...

Physical Processes

- turning and spinning forces.

Check-up

Why is it that some objects float in water and some sink?
How could you make a brick float?

The answer!

Do you remember the question about the snapped carrier bag? Mum had put a lot of heavy things in the bag. The weight of the groceries pulling down was a greater force than the support or pull of the carrier bag and so the handles snapped. Gravity pulled the groceries to the ground. The eggs broke because the force of them hitting the ground made them change shape and break!

6F How we see things

What do you know

- We use our eyes to see.
- Light travels in straight lines from a light source.
- A shadow forms when an opaque object blocks light.
- Some objects reflect light.

What would your life be like without light? Light from the Sun travels at an incredible speed through space to reach us. In this unit we'll find out all about how light behaves and how we receive and interpret it when we see.

Skills check

Can you ...

- make careful observations?
- make and repeat careful measurements?
- collect evidence and see how good it is?
- notice patterns in your results?
- use your evidence to explain what you've found out?
- use your evidence to predict something you don't yet know?

Words to learn

light beam
mirror
opaque
reflect
reflection

Let's find out ...

The Radiation Rangers gang have their base in the shed at the bottom of Philip's garden. Their rivals, the Laser Lads, have their base in the garden next door. How can the Rangers see the Lads approaching before their garden is invaded?

Reflecting light

- We see a light source because light travels from a light source to our eyes.
- Some surfaces reflect light.
- We can represent the path of a beam of light with an arrow.
- When a beam of light is reflected from a surface its direction changes.

Windows on the world

Our eyes are our windows on the world. Light enters our eyes from outside them so that we can see.

We see the Sun, the stars, fireworks and car headlights because they all create and radiate light. Light comes from a source and travels in straight lines at very high speed. Light travels into our eyes. **Light-sensitive** cells at the back of our eyes receive the light and send messages to our brain, which interprets them.

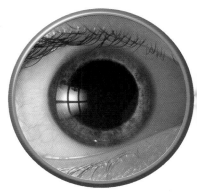

Scattered sunlight

Not everything we see produces its own light. When light hits an object, the object absorbs some of the light energy. The rest either passes straight through the object (if it is transparent, like glass) or bounces back. Light hitting rough surfaces like wood, stone, paper or wool will bounce off them in all directions. We say the light has been scattered.

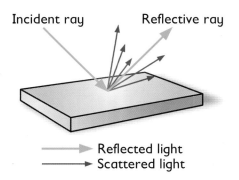

Incident ray   Reflective ray

→ Reflected light
→ Scattered light

On reflection

Polished, smooth or shiny surfaces bounce light rays back in the same direction. That's why we see an image in a mirror.

We see the Moon because it reflects the light from the Sun.

How many things can you think of that reflect light?

Things to do

Make a mirror

- Smooth out a sheet of aluminium foil and use it as a mirror. Can you see your reflection? Now crumple up your foil so that it becomes quite creased. Smooth it out a little. Can you see your face in it? What has happened to your reflection? Why do you think this has happened? Is the foil still reflecting light?

About face

When a beam of light is reflected from a surface, like a mirror, its direction changes.

- Set up a strong light source like an OHP light in a darkened room. Keep your light source still but use a mirror to reflect the light beam to different places in the classroom. What do you notice about the angle of the reflected light beam? Draw what you see. Use PCM 37 to draw the angles of the reflected torch beams.

- When is reflecting light using a mirror be useful?

Digging deeper

**Sound and light
The way we see**

Find out:

- more about the complexity of the human eye and the way we see.
- how to do an investigation into **binocular vision**.

Did you know?

- The focusing muscles around your eyes adjust around 100 000 times every day.

- The Keck telescope in Hawaii has a curved mirror 10 m across to gather the faint light from distant stars.

- American astronauts left a mirror on the Moon to reflect a laser beam sent from Earth 400 000 km away!

I wonder ...

Why are the words 'Police' and 'Ambulance' painted back-to-front on police vehicles and ambulances?

Testing reflective materials

- Find which surface reflects the most light.
- Make careful measurements and observations.
- Generalize from your results.

What to do

Ruth decided to investigate how to make the backyard brighter. She knew that some materials absorbed light and others reflected light. She used the school's computer light sensor to test different materials. How much light did they reflect from a torch beam?

This would be a nice place if it wasn't so dreary. We need to brighten it up a bit.

We could put some lights up, to make it brighter.

Yes, but we can't run electric light out here. We need to lighten the walls and make the most of the sunlight.

What you need

- computer with light sensor attachment
- a selection of materials, e.g. house brick, wallpaper, mirror, white card, black card, corrugated paper, corduroy fabric
- metre rulers
- a torch or strong light source

What to check

Now try it yourselves.

- How will you keep the test fair? How far from the test material should you place your light source? How far should the sensor be from the material?
- How will you record your results? How many readings should you take?
- What do you think will happen?

Ruth made three light sensor readings and took an average of her results. She ranked her results from 'reflected most light' to 'reflected least light'. Here is what she found:

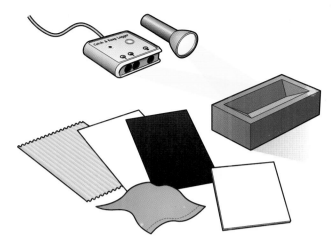

Reflected most light
mirror
white card
corrugated paper
black card
house brick
fabric
Reflected least light

Ruth decided that smooth and shiny surfaces must reflect more light than rough, dull ones. But that didn't explain why the black card didn't reflect much light. Then she noticed that all of the materials that were good reflectors were pale coloured. Perhaps dark materials absorbed more light than pale coloured ones?

Can you do better?

Can you think of more materials to test? How could you improve on Ruth's investigation?

Would the results be the same with a brighter light?

Now predict

- Ruth told her dad about her discoveries and together they made changes to the backyard. Can you suggest other things they could have done and why?

Investigating shadows

- Investigate ways that shadows can change.
- Plan and carry out a fair test.
- Make and check measurements.
- Look for trends in your results.

You shouldn't creep up on people like that.

Didn't you know it was me?

All I could see was a shadow

But shadows are always the same shape as the thing that makes them!

What to do

Kofi and Anna wanted to find out about shadows and how they change.

Shadows are made when light is blocked and are always in the opposite direction to the light source.

You can't see any detail on a shadow.

You can only have shadows in the daytime.

Do you agree with the children? Do you know anything else about shadows and how they are made?

Think of an investigation to measure how a shadow can be changed. Think of as many ideas as you can and choose the idea you like best. Work out how to carry out your investigation.

The children decided to investigate how the angle of the light hitting the object changed the shape of the shadow.

What you need

- a profile of a face cut from card securely mounted on a table
- rulers and metre rules
- a strong light source
- a large board protractor

What to check

Now try it yourselves.

- How are you going to make the test fair? What will you change? What will you keep the same? How will you record your measurements?
- How many times will you repeat your measurements?

What did you find?

The children set up their experiment like this:

They held the torch at different angles. They drew around the shape of the shadow cast on the white board when the torch was held at different angles to the card shape. They measured the length of the shadows at their longest points. Here are their results:

Angle of torch from horizontal (°)	Length of shadow (cm)
10	63
20	45
30	32
40	14
50	11
60	7
70	4.5
80	2
90	0

- They found that the higher the angle of the beam, the shorter the shadow it cast. The lower down they held the torch the longer the shadow appeared. Can you suggest other things that might have changed?

- You could use a computer program to plot this data on a line graph. What do you think the graph will look like? Why?

Can you do better?

If you were doing the same investigation again, is there anything you would do differently? Why? How good is your evidence? Can you see a pattern in your results? Could this be interpreted in more than one way?

Now predict

- When the class were plotting their results on the computer, Janine thought she could see her shadow on the computer screen. Karim said she was wrong and that what she could see was her reflection. How could you decide who was right? What is the difference between a shadow and a reflection?

6F Review

What have you learned?

- Light travels from a source.
- We see light sources when light from them enters our eyes.
- Light from an object can be reflected from a mirror.
- Mirrors can change the direction of a light beam.
- We represent the direction of a ray of light travelling from a light source or reflected from an object by a straight line with an arrow.
- When a beam of light is reflected from a surface its direction changes.
- Shiny surfaces reflect light better than dull surfaces.
- Shiny surfaces can be used as a mirror, dull surfaces cannot.
- Shadows form when light is blocked.
- Changing the position of the light source changes the shadow cast.
- Reflections form when light changes direction off a shiny surface.

Find out more about ...

- how other animals see.
- how lenses change light. Light may be the fastest thing in the universe but it doesn't always travel at the same speed!

Check-up

Why can you see your reflection in a still pool of water but not on the rough sea?

Physical Processes

The answer!

Do you remember the question about how the Radiation Rangers could see the Laser Lads coming? One early warning system would be to mount mirrors on trees to enable the Rangers to 'see around corners'. The images of the Lads would be reflected in the mirrors and then bounced at an angle so that the Rangers could see them. They might also use mirrors to make a periscope to peer over the garden hedge without being seen.

6G Changing circuits

What do you know?

- A complete circuit is needed for electricity to flow and an electrical device to work.
- A switch can be used to make or break a circuit.
- Switches can be used to control electrical devices.
- Metals are good electrical conductors.
- Plastic is a good electrical insulator.
- Mains electricity can be dangerous!

Skills check

Can you ...

- make careful observations?
- make and repeat careful measurements?
- collect evidence and see how good it is?
- notice patterns in your results?
- use your evidence to explain what you've found out?
- use your evidence to predict something you don't yet know?

Words to learn

battery
cell
circuit
circuit diagram
circuit symbol
component
conductor
insulator
resistance
variable resistor

Let's find out ...

In Dr Frankenheimer's sinister laboratory a lifeless body lies on a table. It is connected to an electrical generator by wires. The mad doctor screams in frustration, "I need more power, more power to bring my creation alive! But every time I increase the power the whole system blows up. What am I doing wrong?"

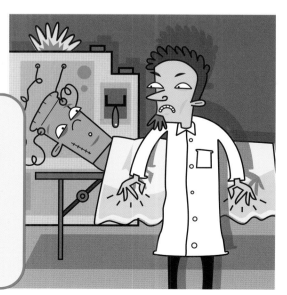

Electrical circuits

- We use symbols to represent components in a circuit.
- Circuit diagrams are used to construct and interpret electrical circuits.
- The performance of components in a circuit can be changed.

Signs and symbols

Look at the care label on an item of clothing. Do you know what the symbols mean? Symbols like these are used as a kind of code to help us understand a lot of information without having to write lots of words. Can you think of other signs and symbols we use in our lives?

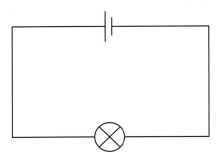

Circuit symbols

Scientists working with electricity use symbols to represent each component in a circuit. The symbols are quick to draw and people all over the world can understand them. You can construct a circuit from a circuit diagram once you know what the symbols mean.

Circuit diagrams

A circuit diagram is a map or plan of an electrical circuit. Follow this circuit diagram to make the circuit.

Now draw a diagram of the circuit in the photo using the correct symbols.

A circuit in series

This circuit has a switch. You can use a circuit diagram to predict whether or not a circuit will work.

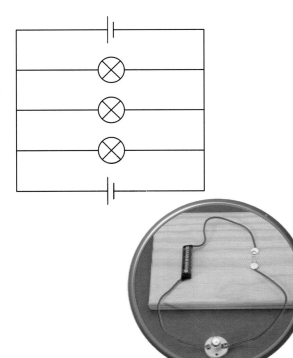

Things to do

Draw a circuit

- Draw a circuit diagram.
- Challenge a friend to construct a circuit using the diagram you have drawn. How quickly can they do it?
- Are all the components in the right place? Now swap roles. How many different circuits can you make and draw? Do all of them work?

How bright?

Look at these circuit diagrams.

- Use your knowledge to predict which circuit will be brightest.
- Now make the circuits – were you correct?

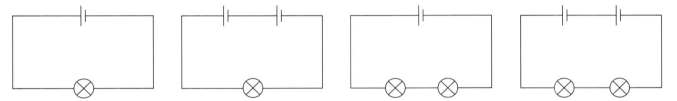

Digging deeper

Electricity and magnetism
Circuits

Find out:

- more about circuits.

Did you know?

- Thousands of tiny electrical circuits called microcircuits can be built on tiny silicon computer chips.
- The voltage of domestic electricity is about 230 V and this can kill you. However, in 1967 an American survived an electric shock of 230 000 V.

I wonder ...

What is a 'short circuit' and why can it be dangerous?

Testing wires

Your challenge

- Find if the length of the wire in a circuit affects the brightness of the bulb.
- Make careful measurements and observations.

What to do

We can change the brightness of a bulb in a circuit by adding or taking away batteries. Think of other ways we might alter how bright a bulb is.

Does the length of wire make a difference?

Does the wire always have to be copper?

How about changing the thickness of the wire?

This wire doesn't have plastic coating so we can't use that can we?

Do you have any other ideas?

The children decided to investigate how the length of the wire affected the brightness of the bulb in a circuit. They used thin nichrome wire mounted between two screws on a long piece of wood. They marked the board at 10 cm intervals and used crocodile clips to join the wire into their circuit.

The first observation they made was without the thin wire. Why did they do that?

What you need

- nichrome wire
- metre rule
- batteries
- bulb
- connecting wire
- computer with light sensor

What to check

Now try it yourselves.

- How will you keep the test fair? How will you judge the brightness of the bulb?
- How many readings should you take?
- How will you make sure that your components are matched?

What did you find?

Length of fuse wire in circuit (cm)	Brightness of bulb
0	extremely bright
10	very bright
20	bright
30	bright
40	fairly dim
50	dim
60	cannot see any light

The children in Class 6 used two batteries in their circuit and moved the crocodile clips along the wire at regular intervals to increase the length of wire in the circuit. As they did this, they noticed changes in the brightness of their bulb.

- The children decided that the longer the wire the dimmer the bulb. Do you agree with their result?

- Can you explain what is happening to the current in the circuit? Why does the bulb get dimmer?

Can you do better?

How could you improve on Class 6's investigation?

Would the results be the same if you used a different thickness of wire?

Is there a better way of judging the brightness of the bulb?

Is there another way of measuring how the current in the circuit changes?

Now predict

- At teatime, when Ross got home from school, he told his Mum about what he'd learned in science that day.

That's interesting. So the longer the wire the dimmer the bulbs. Hang on! There are hundreds of metres of wiring in this flat. Why don't we have some light bulbs that are brighter than others?

Electrical resistance

Things to learn

- Resistance is how easily electricity passes through materials in a circuit.
- Different materials have different levels of resistance.
- You can change the resistance in a circuit.

Resistance

Good electrical conductors, like metal and graphite allow electricity to pass through them quite easily. We say they have low electrical resistance. Other materials have high resistance and we call them electrical insulators. Materials like plastic and rubber have high electrical resistance.

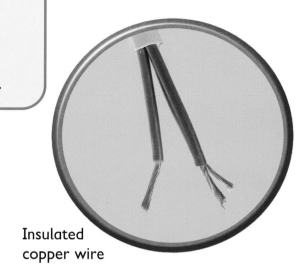

Insulated
copper wire

More means less!

You'll remember that electric current is the flow of electrons through a conductor. In any circuit, the strength of the current depends upon the resistance of the components in it. Components that are resistant will weaken the flow of electricity.

Adding components in a series circuit (components in a straight line) will increase the resistance in the circuit; bulbs will become dimmer as more of them are added, motors will become slower, buzzers quieter.

Which wire?

Copper wires are used in houses because copper has a low electrical resistance and allows the electrical current to flow through it easily. Nichrome wire has a much greater resistance and doesn't allow electricity to pass through it as easily. The length of copper wire in a circuit doesn't affect the flow of mains electricity but long nichrome or resistance wires in a circuit have greater resistance than shorter wires.

If you use a thick wire, it is like a wider water pipe. A bulb will glow more brightly with a thick wire than with a thin wire.

Things to do

Varying the resistance

Sometimes we want to change the resistance in a circuit deliberately. We use a variable resistor to do this. For example, we use **dimmer switches** to turn down lights or a volume control to increase the volume on a radio or tape recorder. With a dimmer switch or volume control, when you turn the control the variable resistor changes the resistance in the circuit and the amount of electricity flowing through the device.

Batteries are safe and portable

- Make your own variable resistor by connecting the graphite lead from the inside of a pencil into your circuit. As graphite has a higher electrical resistance than the copper wires in your circuit, you can change the resistance by changing the length of graphite you use.

Circuit with a variable resistor

Digging deeper

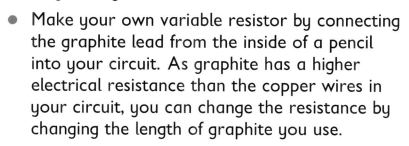

Electricity and magnetism
Electricity on the move

Find out:

- more about resistance and changing circuits.

Did you know?

- The filament of a light bulb is made from tungsten which glows without burning when electricity passes through it.

- The volume control on a personal stereo is a variable resistor. It changes the length of wire in the circuit. The shorter the wire the louder the sound.

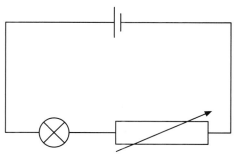

I wonder ...

Why do we have fuses in domestic appliances and how do they work?

6G Review

Find out more about ...

Physical Processes

- circuit breakers and fuses.
- Michael Faraday, who first produced electricity as long ago as 1831. You can also find out about the electricity of the future.

Check-up

Steven got an electric racing car set for his birthday. He can control the speed of the cars by squeezing the trigger on the control unit. What do you think is happening to the current in the circuit? How does the speed controller work?

The answer!

Do you remember the question about the mad scientist who couldn't get his machine to work?

Electricity can be useful to doctors using machines called defibrillators. These give a carefully controlled electric shock to start a person's heart beating again if it has stopped after a heart attack. However, passing electricity through a person as Dr Frankenheimer is trying to do would probably kill them. The doctor's machine might not work for many reasons – perhaps he is trying to pass too much electrical current through wires or components that aren't strong enough for the power source and so the wires melt.

5/6H Enquiry in context

What do you know?

- Habitats differ.
- Different plants and animals grow in different habitats.
- Plants and animals are adapted to their environment.
- A full circuit is needed for electricity to flow.
- Some materials conduct electricity easily.
- A switch can be used to control the flow of electricity in a circuit.
- How to plan and carry out an investigation.

Skills check

Can you ...

- make careful observations and measurements?
- collect evidence and see how good it is?
- use your evidence to explain what you've found out?
- use your evidence to predict something you don't yet know?

Words to learn

adaptation   conductor

annotate   data

burglar   insulator
alarm
                sample
complete
circuit   switch

                trend

Let's find out ...

"Look at all the caterpillars under these leaves," said Aunt Louise to the children. "They are all lined up – and all munching away." "Why aren't there caterpillars on top of the leaves?" asked Aunt Louise.

"There are," said Simon. "But there aren't as many." "How do you know?" said his sister. "Because I've looked," said Simon. "Have you looked at all the leaves on the tree?" said Aunt Louise. "Of course not," said Simon. "Just how many leaves should we look at?"

Dandelions

Your challenge

- Decide how to answer a scientific question.
- Decide what evidence to collect.
- Handle your data correctly.
- Explain your results from what you know about science.
- Decide just how good your evidence is.

"I've found a new dandelion plant!" called Martin from the edge of the school field. "How is it different from mine?" asked Fitzroy from the middle of the field. "Mine is tall – yours are flat." "Do you think they're the same plant?" said Fitzroy. "I don't know," said Martin. "I think I need to look at more plants to tell."

Martin and Fitzroy decided to find whether dandelions were taller by the hedge than in the middle of the field. They decided to count 20 each.

What to do

Look in a field, a garden or a park. Find a dandelion that is growing near the middle of the field. Find another that is growing near the edge – by a hedge or under a tree. Draw both dandelions. Next to each picture, list the differences you can see.

Now sample more dandelions in both places. How many are like your picture of each dandelion?

What you need

- your pictures
- a ruler

What to check

Now try it yourselves.

- Look for a sample number of dandelions (you can't do them all!).
- Measure the dandelions and record them. Look for a pattern in your results.

What did you find?

Martin and Fitzroy recorded their results in a table.

Number of flat dandelions in the field	Number of tall dandelions in the field	Number of flat dandelions near the hedge	Number of tall dandelions near the hedge
20	0	3	17

The boys were confident in their results. Flat dandelions grew in the middle of the field, tall ones by the hedge.

- Why do you think the boys got these results? Are they like yours?
- How do you explain them?

Maybe dandelions in the middle of the field get trodden flat!

No, I think it's darker by the hedge. Dandelions in the middle of the field get more Sun. That's why they are different shapes!

Can you do better?

Are the dandelions two different plants – 'field' dandelions and 'border' dandelions? Swap their positions to help you find out.

Use a washed can without a lid and no sharp edges. Tread the can in around a dandelion in the field. Pull it up, together with its core of soil, and swap it with a dandelion in the hedge. Mark and water your plants. Then wait and see what happens!

Now predict

- Children at another school compared grasses growing across a well-trodden path with grasses growing in a field. They looked at the length of the leaves. What do you think they discovered?

Burglar alarm

Your challenge

- Plan a burglar alarm using your knowledge of science.
- Test your design.
- Improve your design so that it works better.
- Explain how your design works.
- Evaluate your design, and other people's.

What to do

Tina was reading a book about burglars. 'Protect your door with a pressure switch,' it said. Pressure switches work when two conductors are brought together to complete a circuit. They are separated by a squashy insulating material like sponge. Holes in the sponge should allow the two conductors to make contact. 'I'll make one of those!' thought Tina. 'I'll use cooking foil for the conductors. But what's best for the insulator?'

'Maybe I could use carpet,' she thought. 'Or thin rubber. Or foam. As long as the conductors can touch, it will make a switch. I'll have to wire it into a circuit.'

What else will Tina need to make a complete circuit? What will the switch operate? A bulb – or a buzzer?

What you need

- cooking foil
- a thin squashy insulator
- several wires
- a bulb in a bulb-holder or a buzzer
- a battery

What to check

Now try it yourselves.

- Will the circuit be complete when a burglar treads on it?
- You need to make holes in the insulator. But how many holes – and where?

What did you find?

Tina's switch only worked when really heavy people trod on it. She decided to write a complete evaluation. Her evaluation looked like this:

My pressure switch

GOOD POINTS

It's quite small. It will fit under a doormat.

It's got good connections.

It's quite nice to look at. I've decorated it.

BAD POINTS

It only works with heavy burglars.

My battery is old. It's nearly flat.

IMPROVEMENTS

I need to get a thinner insulator, or make more holes.

I need a new battery.

Can you do better?

Tina told people about her burglar alarm. "How does it work?" they asked.

Tina should have drawn a picture of her pressure switch. She could have annotated her picture.

- Draw a picture of your pressure switch.
- Make notes about how it works.
- Write an evaluation of your switch.

Now predict

- Tina couldn't find a thin enough insulator so she took it out altogether. What happened to the switch?

Dandelions and burglar alarms

Things to learn

- Understand the question you are answering.
- Make the right observations and measurements.
- Understand the data you have collected.
- Use scientific words correctly.
- Have ideas of how to improve your work.

Sample size

In an enquiry like this, **sample size** is important. If you only pull one leaf from each place and compare them, you may have the start of an idea. You can only be more sure about it if you consider a big enough sample. But how big? Suppose you only measure all the largest leaves you can see? Suppose you pick from a shady edge rather than one in full Sun? Is that fair?

The skills you use

Enquiry is a large part of both the dandelion and the alarm activities. Information-processing is also very important. Discuss how you select your dandelions, and what you can do to improve failing burglar alarms. Compare different ideas and think about how to improve. Be brave enough to try out something new. Always remember to evaluate your work. That way you will learn from it - and get new ideas!

Things to do

Dandelions

You might decide to record leaf size and length.

- Use a computer program to help you compare your data. Create graphs of leaf sizes for dandelions found in a certain area. You don't have to choose dandelions. You might compare the height of sunflowers in different places; leaf sizes up and down a shrub; pond life at different water levels; insects on the top and underside of leaves; new plants on a patch of bare ground. To these you might add changes in plant life across a well-trodden path; the opening of daisy flowers at different times of the day, or the flowering of plants with bulbs.

Burglar alarms

You might have ideas for a door or window sensor; an alarm operated by breaking a **magnetic field** using a tiny, magnetically-operated reed switch; or an alarm triggered by moving something.

- Make a tilt switch by wrapping a Plasticine ball in kitchen foil. Put it in a film canister with two terminals at the end. Or find ways of protecting a chocolate bar (which can be seen by everyone) from theft!

- Examine ready-made pressure pads. See what materials they are made from and how they are constructed.

Exploring

Electricity
What is electricity?

Find out:

- more about how electricity travels.

Did you know?

- You can eat dandelions in salads. In some countries, they are grown as a crop. They taste peppery.

- What else eats dandelions?

I wonder ...
How does a house burglar alarm system work? What does the alarm sense?

5/6H Review

What have you learned?

- How to answer a scientific question.
- What evidence to collect.
- How to handle your data correctly.
- Explaining your results from what you know of science.
- Deciding just how good your evidence is.
- Planning a burglar alarm using your knowledge of science.
- Testing your design.
- Improving your design so that it works better.
- Explaining how your design works.
- Evaluating your design, and other people's.

Find out more about ...

Physical Processes

- what happens when electricity flows.

Check-up

"Everybody's got a bike except me!" said Duncan. "Who's everybody?" asked his mum. "Alan and Jordan," said Duncan. "They're not everybody," said his mum.

Was she right? What has this got to do with sample size? What must Duncan do to prove that he has been missed out?

The answer!

Remember the first question about how many leaves to look at? 'Enough!' is the answer. One leaf isn't enough – but a whole tree is more than Simon could manage. He and his sister need to decide on a sensible sample size. Twenty leaves, perhaps – or 50?

6A Interdependence and adaptation checklist

Think about these statements.

Which do you know? Which can you do?

- I can recognize some animals in a habitat.
- I can observe some living organisms.
- I know that animals need food to survive.
- I know that mice are found in fields and seaweed is found in the sea.
- I know that a fish has fins to swim and that a cactus has a thick stem to store water.
- I can measure the amount a plant grows.
- I can use a key to identify plants and animals.
- I can write a simple food chain to show eating patterns.
- I know a predator eats other animals.
- I can plot my data into a bar chart and explain what it means.
- I know that willow trees are found in wet ground because there is more water there.
- I know that some plants can survive with less light so don't need to grow as tall in a rainforest.
- I can plot my data into a line graph and explain which conditions the plant grew best in.

6B Micro-organisms checklist

What do you know?

Think about these statements.

Which do you know? Which can you do?

- I can describe a living organism.
- I can tell you what I observe.
- I know that all living organisms grow and reproduce.
- I know what a microbe needs to grow.
- I can make and record regular observations of my bread mould.
- I can explain why dry, cold bread didn't grow mould.
- I can measure the circumference of the balloon inflation in the yeast activity.
- I know that we can't live without microbes.
- I can explain why the yeast in hot water didn't produce carbon dioxide.
- I can plot a bar chart of my results.
- I know to change only one factor when investigating making bread.
- I can suggest that repeating an investigation, perhaps by putting more than one piece of bread in the same conditions, gives more reliable results.
- I can explain how Jenner tested vaccination, or how Pasteur discovered that a living organism is involved in fermentation.

6C More about dissolving checklist

What do you know?

Think about these statements.

Which do you know? Which can you do?

- I can describe a material by colour and texture.

- I can tell you what I observe.

- I can identify a range of materials, like water, wood and air.

- I can use a stopwatch.

- I can put my results in a table.

- I know that some solids dissolve.

- I know that you can separate a liquid from a solid.

- I can measure the volume of a liquid.

- I know how to filter a solid from a liquid.

- I know how to evaporate a liquid from a solution to leave the solid.

- I know when to repeat my observations and measurements.

- I can plot a bar chart of my results.

- I can separate salt and water, or produce clean water from a muddy puddle.

- I know that rain is part of the water cycle.

- I can explain why I should repeat measurements and observations.

- I can plot a line graph of my results.

6D Reversible and irreversible changes checklist

Think about these statements.

Which do you know? Which can you do?

- I can tell you what I observe when I watch a candle burning.
- I know the properties of solids, liquids and gases.
- I can sort solids, liquids and gases and tell you the reasons for my classification.
- I can explain to you what happens when materials burn.
- I can tell you why burning is not a reversible change.
- I can describe the products of burning.
- I can make general statements about my observations.
- I can explain my observations.
- I can explain how solids, liquids and gases are different.
- I can select the equipment I need and use it effectively.
- I can suggest ways of improving my work.
- I can explain how evaporation and condensation affect some waste products from burning.
- I can suggest why repeating an enquiry gives more reliable results.
- I can draw conclusions that match my evidence.
- I can explain how some famous scientists used enquiry skills.

6E Forces in action checklist

What do you know?

Think about these statements.

Which do you know? Which can you do?

- I can make observations of the way things move.
- I can describe the effects of friction and gravity on something I am trying to move.
- I can compare the differences in test results between two or more falling objects.
- I can predict accurately whether something will sink or float.
- I can compare differences in frictional forces, for example, how something moves over different surfaces.
- I can explain how different conditions lead to different frictional effects.
- I can make changes to falling or floating objects and predict what the out come is likely to be.
- I can choose the right forcemeter for a task and make accurate forcemeter readings.
- I can explain my scientific enquiry results.
- I can make a general statement.
- I can use arrows correctly to record the direction and size of forces.
- I can explain how gravity works to draw things together, and how the gravity of the Earth results in things falling towards it.
- I can explain why things sink and float, making use of ideas about upthrust.
- I can tell you about real world examples of the use of gravity and floating.

6F How we see things checklist

Think about these statements.

Which do you know? Which can you do?

- I can describe my investigations of light correctly.
- I know how to change the direction of reflected light.
- I can use a simple table and the correct vocabulary to record my discoveries.
- I can describe how light is reflected from a mirror.
- I know why it is important to record discoveries.
- I know why it is important to keep some things the same while changing others in an investigation.
- I can see the patterns in my results and give reasons for them.
- I can make statements like "shiny surfaces reflect light better than dull surfaces".
- I can record my results in a table and transfer it to a graph.
- I can explain what I found out, and how to do it better.
- I can explain to you how mirrors reflect images.
- I can tell you how good my evidence is, and why.
- I can suggest further investigations following my discoveries.
- I can tell you how and why images are changed by reflection in a mirror.

6G Changing circuits checklist

What do you know?

Think about these statements.

Which do you know? Which can you do?

- I can show you how to make a simple circuit, either by talking to you or by drawing a picture.

- I can make up a simple circuit and explain to you what I have done.

- I can use electrical components to make up simple circuits and tell you whether my predictions about them were correct.

- I can compare the way that bulbs work in different electrical circuits.

- I can carry out a fair test – e.g. of insulators and conductors, or of changes in an electrical circuit – and suggest ways of doing it better.

- I can explain to you the reason why a bulb does not light, because there is a break in the circuit or the switch is open.

- I can represent my circuit as a drawing.

- I can choose components to add to my circuits, predict what they will do, and explain what happened when I added them.

- I can tell you how to put a buzzer or motor into an electric circuit, and how to control it with a switch.

- I can use symbols correctly to represent my circuit.

- I can make a circuit from a diagram of conventional symbols.

- I know how altering the current in my circuit can affect the brightness of bulbs.

- I can explain why the brightness of the bulbs varies.

5/6H Enquiry in context checklist

What do you know?

Think about these statements.

Which do you know? Which can you do?

- I can describe two different dandelions.
- I can describe differences in electrical circuits.
- I can tell you what I observe.
- I know that all living organisms grow and reproduce.
- I know how to make up an electrical circuit.
- I can compare two different dandelions.
- I can plan a burglar alarm with help.
- I can suggest why habitat conditions could affect the growth of plants.
- I can link cause and effect, e.g. "standing on my pressure pad completes the circuit".
- I can make general statements about my enquiries.
- I can explain my observations.
- I can explain from my scientific knowledge why two dandelions might differ in shape.
- I can explain how my burglar alarm circuit works.
- I can select the equipment I need and use it effectively.
- I can suggest ways of improving my work.
- I can suggest why repeating an enquiry gives more reliable results.
- I can draw conclusions that match my evidence.
- I can explain how some famous scientists used enquiry skills.

Glossary

air – the gas

anchor – holding in place to stop from floating away

astronaut – space explorer

bacteria – single cell micro-organisms

a line of best fit – the closest line to the points on a graph

binocular vision – seeing with two eyes

biotechnology – using living organisms to make food, medicines and other products

burnt – changed completely and irreversibly by fire

camouflage – the natural colour or shape of an animal which enables it to blend with its surroundings

ceramic – material made from clay at very high temperatures

chemical reaction – when two or more chemicals come together to make a change and produce new substances

colony – a collection of millions of bacteria that may be visible as a coloured spot

compost – plant material rotted by bacteria, used as a fertilizer

control – unchanged part of a science investigation

cornflour – finely ground maize flour

decant – to pour off a liquid slowly leaving the undissolved solid behind

decay – to rot

descent – to travel down

dimmer switch – alters the brightness of light by variable resistance

escape velocity – the speed at which an object will need to travel to escape a planet's gravity

eyesight – the ability to see

filtration – separating the solution and an undissolved solid using a fine sieve

glide – to move with a smooth continuous motion

gravity – the pull of any object on another

holdfast – the anchor of a seaweed

hydroponics – growing plants in sand, gravel, or water, without soil but with added nutrients

indigestion powder – medicine to treat difficulty in digesting food

Jupiter – the fifth planet from the Sun and the largest in the solar system

light sensitive – responds to the level of light it is subjected to

lubricating oil – oil that reduces friction between surfaces

magnetic field – area round a magnet where its force can be felt

Mars – fourth planet from the Sun, called the red planet

mucus – slime that lubricates and protects

parachutist – person who flies a parachute

parasite – plant or animal that lives off another

photosynthesis – how green plants trap light energy and use it to make food

plaster of Paris – a white powder made from gypsum and mixed with water to make casts and moulds

preserved – kept unchanged

rock pool – saltwater pond left behind by the tide

rotor – spinning wing or propeller

sample size – the selection you make when you can't count everything

saturated – a solution so full it can't dissolve any more solid

sludge – thick greasy residue

solute – a solid dissolved in a liquid

solvent – the liquid a solid dissolves in

soot – a black material that rises in smoke

starch – a sugary material in which form plants store their food

suspension – tiny pieces of a solid spread undissolved through a liquid

trend – a pattern of results showing a general direction or tendency

tropical rainforest – dense, hot, wet forest near the equator

upthrust – the upward push of water that helps boats float

velocity – the speed of something in one direction

waterlogged – saturated with water

weight – the force of gravity on an object, depending on its mass

wick – a thread that feeds the candle flame with fuel